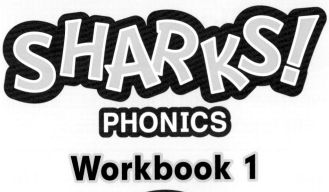

SHARKS!

PHONICS

Workbook 1

By Quinlan B. Lee

Photo Credits: cover: Watt Jim/Getty Images; title page: solarseven/Shutterstock; page 2: Brian J. Skerry/Getty Images, Water Frame/ Alamy, Norbert Probst/Corbis, Becca Saunders/Minden Pictures, page 3: Matt9122/Shutterstock; page 5: Dimitri Otis/Getty Images; page 7: Jim Abernethy/National Geographic; page 8: Watt Jim/Getty Images, Greg Amptman/Shutterstock; page 9: Dan Callister/ Alamy; page 11: Mike Parry/Minden Pictures; page 12: James Watt/Getty Images; page 13: qidian/iStockphoto; page 15: Dan Callister/ Alamy; page 16: Watt Jim/Getty Images, Greg Amptman/Shutterstock

No part of this publication may be reproduced, stored in a retrieval system, or transmitted in any form or by any means, electronic, mechanical, photocopying, recording, or otherwise, without written permission of the publisher. For information regarding permission, write to Scholastic Inc., Attention: Permissions Department, 557 Broadway, New York, NY, 10012.

Copyright © 2014 by Scholastic Inc. All rights reserved. Published by Scholastic Inc. SCHOLASTIC and associated logos are trademarks and/or registered trademarks of Scholastic Inc.

ISB

12 11 10 9 8 7 6 5 4 3 2 1

P

D1092615

First Printing, September

SCHOLASTIC INC.

Fill in the Blanks

Sharks live in every ocean in the world. Fill in the blanks with *sh* words to learn other **shark** facts.

shoe	sharp	ship	shovel

Whale sharks are as big as a

_____.

Pygmy sharks are as small as a

_____.

Hammerhead shark snouts are shaped

like a _____.

Longnose saw sharks have a long

nose with _____ teeth.

Make New Words

Sharks come in all different **shapes**. Words come in all different **shapes**, too. Change one letter in the *sh* words below to make a new word. Use the word clues to help you.

s h a r k	s h a r _____	pointy like teeth
s h a p e	s h a _____ e	to give to someone else
s h o t	s h o _____	you wear it on your foot
s h o r e	s h o r _____	not tall

Hidden Words

There are hidden **sh** words in the puzzle below. Can you find them? Look for the words in the box and circle them.

share   shine   ship   shoe

sharks   shallow   shovel

q s h a r k s

s h a l l o w

h o e s h o e

a v s h i n e

r e m i t h s

e l b p a c l

Match the Rhymes

Fresh fish is a shark's favorite **dish**. **Fish** and **dish** rhyme. Draw lines to match the other words that rhyme.

crash   dish

fish   smash

flush   blush

squish   flash

splash   crush

brush   swish

Add the Blend

A **shark** is a **fish**. **Shark** starts with the **sh** sound. **Fish** ends with the **sh** sound. Fill in **sh** at the beginning or end to complete the words below. Then read the words aloud.

fre_____   cra_____

_____allow   _____ows

squi_____   bru_____

_____ore   swi_____

fla_____   _____ape

_____ine   _____ovel

Mixed-up Words

Check out this shark's teeth! **Chomp!**
Now **check** out these words! They are all mixed-up. Draw lines to connect the scrambled *ch* words to their correct spelling on the right.

ercahg   chase

ohcw   chew

esahc   chunks

hwec   charge

nchega   chow

nskchu   change

Chase the Prey

Sharks are predators. They **chase** other animals to eat them. Help this shark **chase** its prey by coloring the words that begin with the *ch* sound.

	chase	chomp	check	shark	fish
eat	prey	crabs	charge	chose	one
smell	off	sandy	clock	chunks	swim
teeth	sneak	chew	chow	change	can
want	catch	chop	close	get	shore
make	steal	chock	chum	choose	

Find the Rhymes

After shark eggs **hatch**, predators try to **snatch** the new pups. **Hatch** and **snatch** rhyme. In the rows below, put an X through the word that does not rhyme.

1. hatch   crash   patch

2. snatch   beach   teach

3. bunch   swish   hunch

4. reach   each   chomp

Unscramble the Sentences

Shark pups are born many different ways. Unscramble the sentences below to find out facts about different shark pups.

1. mom. hatch inside eggs Hammerhead their

_____

_____

2. 100 time. sharks Whale a have pups at

_____

_____

3. beach. born near Lemon pups shark are the

_____

_____

Complete the Sentences

Shark **teeth** are sharp and can chew almost anything.
Fill in the correct **th** word below to find out more about
shark **teeth**.

Sharks have five rows of _____.

> teeth   tooth

Some sharks have three _____ teeth.

> mouth   thousand

Sharks are always growing new _____.

> think   teeth

Beginning or Ending?

Sharks catch all sorts of **things** with their **teeth** like coats, paint cans, even bikes! The word **things** starts with the *th* sound and **teeth** ends with the *th* sound. Draw a circle around the words that begin with *th* like **things**. Draw a box around the words that end with *th* like **teeth**.

mouth	three	two	spot
hatch	cloth	thirty	rows
thousand	think	crash	sixth
sixty	hundred	through	tooth

Word Scrambles

These words about sharks are all scrambled. Unscramble the letters and write the word on the lines. Use the clues to help you.

sharks' favorite food

shif   ____ ____ ____ ____

when a pup comes out of its egg

htahc   ____ ____ ____ ____ ____

shark bones don't break, they do this

ssiuqh   ____ ____ ____ ____ ____ ____

size of a pygmy shark

eohs   ____ ____ ____ ____

chunks of fish that attract sharks

mhcu   ____ ____ ____ ____

Complete the Words

The words below are missing their beginning or ending sounds. Add **sh**, **ch**, or **th** to complete the word. Use the clues if you need a hint.

_____allow   not deep

_____ew   to cut up with teeth

cra____   to run into

snat_____   to grab quickly

mou____   where you find teeth

____ase   to go after

____arp   pointy

bea_____   place with sand and water

____ink   what you do with your brain

Word Search

Look in the puzzle below to find the words in the box.

shape	flash	fresh	change
chomp	bunch	pouch	thirty

c	a	n	n	a	x	m	a	s	l
h	a	r	k	p	r	f	c	o	o
o	b	u	f	l	a	s	h	i	j
m	u	s	e	b	s	h	a	p	e
p	o	u	c	h	b	u	n	c	h
t	h	i	r	t	y	a	g	s	h
i	r	t	y	h	f	r	e	s	h

Answer Key

p. 2
ship, shoe, shovel, sharp

p. 3
sharp, share, shoe, short

p. 4

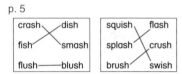

```
q  s  h  a  r  k  s
s  h  a  l  l  o  w
h  o  e  s  h  o  e
a  v  s  h  i  n  e
r  e  m  i  t  h  s
e  l  b  p  a  c  l
```

p. 5

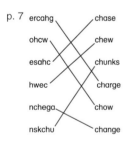

```
crash    dish        squish    flash
fish     smash       splash    crush
flush —— blush       brush     swish
```

p. 6
Column 1: fresh, shallow,
squish, shore, flash, shine
Column 2: crash, shows,
brush, swish, shape, shovel

p. 7
```
ercahg          chase
ohcw            chew
esahc           chunks
hwec            charge
nchega          chow
nskchu          change
```

p. 8

	chase	chomp	check	shark	fish
eat	prey	crabs	charge	chose	one
smell	off	sandy	clock	chunks	swim
teeth	sneak	chew	chow	change	can
want	catch	chop	close	get	shore
make	steal	chock	chum	choose	

p. 9 1. hatch   ~~crash~~   patch

2. ~~snatch~~   beach   teach

3. bunch   ~~swish~~   hunch

4. reach   each   ~~chomp~~

p. 10
1. Hammerhead eggs hatch inside their mom.
2. Whale sharks have 100 pups at a time.
3. Lemon shark pups are born near the beach.

p. 11
teeth, thousand, teeth

p. 12

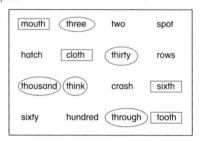

```
mouth    three    two      spot

hatch    cloth    thirty   rows

thousand think    crash    sixth

sixty    hundred  through  tooth
```

p. 13
fish, hatch, squish, shoe, chum

p. 14
shallow, chew, crash, snatch, mouth, chase,
sharp, beach, think

p. 15

```
c  a  n  n  a  x  m  a  s  l
h  a  r  k  p  r  f  c  o  o
o  b  u  f  l  a  s  h  i  j
m  u  s  e  b  s  h  a  p  e
p  o  u  c  h  b  u  n  c  h
t  h  i  r  t  y  a  g  s  h
i  r  t  y  h  f  r  e  s  h
```